SESAME STREET

Working Together

MY FIRST MANNERS

Written by Catherine Lukas

Illustrated by Joe Ewers

Published by Phoenix International Publications, Inc.
8501 West Higgins Road, Suite 300, Chicago, Illinois 60631
Lower Ground Floor, 59 Gloucester Place, London W1U 8JJ

www.pikidsmedia.com

p i kids is a trademark of Phoenix International Publications, Inc., and is registered in the United States.

8 7 6 5 4 3 2 1

ISBN: 978-1-4127-6781-1

 phoenix international publications, inc.